ANNA DEL CONTE'S
Italian Kitchen
GLI ANTIPASTI

ANTIPASTI AND OTHER APPETIZERS

ILLUSTRATED BY FLO BAYLEY

SIMON &
SCHUSTER

SIMON & SCHUSTER

SIMON & SCHUSTER
Simon & Schuster Building
Rockefeller Center
1230 Avenue of the Americas
New York, New York 10020

Copyright © 1993 Pavilion Books
Text copyright © 1993 Anna del Conte
Illustrations copyright © 1993 Flo Bayley

Designed by Andrew Barron & Collis Clements Associates

Printed in Italy by New Interlitho, Milan

10 9 8 7 6 5 4 3 2 1

Library of Congress Cataloging in Publication Data:
Del Conte, Anna.
  Gli antipasti : antipasti and other appetizers / by Anna
del Conte.
      p.   cm. — (Anna del Conte's Italian kitchen)
  Includes bibliographical references and index.
  ISBN 0–671–87029–7 : $14.00
  1. Appetizers.   2. Cookery, Italian.   I. Title.
II. Series: Del Conte, Anna.   Anna del Conte's Italian
kitchen.
TX740.D463   1993
641.8'12—dc20   93–13389
                                                              CIP

CONTENTS

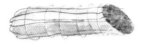

GLI ANTIPASTI

When I was taken out to dinner as a child, I only ate *l'antipasto*. The trolley would be wheeled next to me and I would be transfixed by the beauty of the food and bewildered by the choice. After a few decades I still feel like that. I want to take all the dishes home, admire them, and eat them slowly and thoughtfully over the next few days. First a taste of prosciutto, as well as culatello and felino, my favorite salami, which I would eat with bread and nothing else. Next would come a few floppy slices of grilled bell peppers, a curly tentacle of *calameretti*, and a morsel of each stuffed vegetable. Finally, a spoonful of *nervetti in insalata* – Milanese head cheese – gleaming with olive oil and crowned with colorful *sottaceti* – vegetables preserved in vinegar – and speckled with purple olives and miniscule green capers.

Such are the delights of an antipasto offered in a restaurant. When you serve antipasti at home, however, you must be more selective and decide on two or three dishes at most. Otherwise you will be in the kitchen far too long and begin to hate the idea of an antipasto altogether.

An antipasto can provide a good beginning to a meal, and it can even set the style for the meal itself. It is very important that, as an opening to the meal, it should be well presented and pretty to look at. It should also be light and fresh, so as to develop the taste buds for the courses to follow, rather than fill the stomach, and it should harmonize with the rest of the meal.

Nowadays an antipasto is usually an appetizer, no longer followed by a *primo* – first course – except on special occasions. For instance, if you have decided on a platter of *affettato misto* – mixed cured meats – a generous bowl of tagliatelle dressed with a vigorous sauce would make an ideal follow-on. So, too, would an earthy risotto or a gutsy spaghetti *alla puttanesca* – with tomatoes, anchovies, and chili pepper. This is not the traditional Italian way, but it is what suits our smaller stomachs and the preachings of the health gurus.

If, however, you are serving a roast, start with a vegetable-based antipasto or a fish one. A fish antipasto, indeed, is the ideal precursor to a fish main course.

The recipes collected here are divided into six sections: Salumi, Various Salads, Fish and Meat Antipasti, Stuffed Vegetables, Crostini and Bruschetta, and Other Favorites. Some of the recipes are for classic antipasto dishes, others are my own or those of my family and friends. All are typically Italian yet very varied. As varied, indeed, as most Italian cooking, because of the great differences between its many regions.

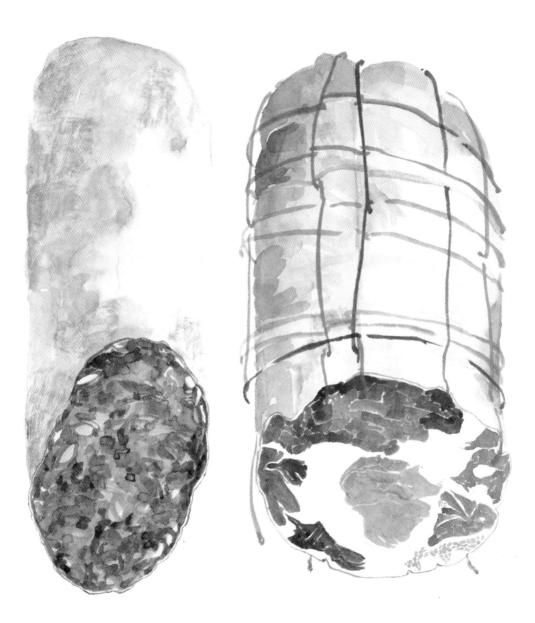

SALUMI

I know I am an unashamed chauvinist where food is concerned, but I am sure no other country offers such an array of delectable cured meats as Italy does. Salumi are usually made with pork or a mixture of pork and beef. There are also good salumi made with venison and various other meats. The mocetta from Valle d'Aosta is made with wild goat, the bresaola from Valtellina with beef tenderloin, the salame d'oca from Friuli and Veneto with goose, and the salami and prosciutti di cinghiale are made with wild boar. This latter is one of the many glories of Tuscany.

The characteristics of the many types of salumi are determined firstly by factors affecting the pig, or other animal, itself. These include its bread, its habitat and food, and the climate of the locality in which it is reared. A prosciutto di Parma is paler and sweeter than, for instance, a prosciutto di montagna – mountain prosciutto. Secondly, salumi differ according to which cuts of meat are used, the proportion of fat to lean, the fineness of the grinding the flavorings, and the curing.

In what follows I describe some of the salumi that I like to serve as an antipasto. Together they form a dish called *affettato misto*, possibly the most common antipasto served in Italy. This dish of mixed cured meats is pretty to look at in its shades of pink and red, and one of the most appetizing ways to start a meal.

You may be serving the *affettato* before a dish of pasta. (This is where I should point out that the word antipasto does *not* mean before the pasta. It means before the "*pasto*" – meal.) In Italy, however, *affettato* is often served as a *secondo* for lunch, not before but after the pasta which is de riguer (only for lunch, though) in any self-respecting Italian family. Still, *primo* or *secondo, affettato misto* is an excellent dish, which, with some good bread or a piece of focaccia, followed by a lovely green salad and some cheese, is a perfect meal in its own right.

A good *affettato misto* should have a choice of at least five or six different meats. The following is a list of the products you can most easily find in this country. You can mix them to your liking, but one type of prosciutto and two types of salami would always be included. With a prosciutto I put two or three different kinds of salami: one from northern Italy, a Milano perhaps, which is mild and sweet, a peppery salame from the south, and a Roman oval-shaped soppressata. An alternative that I like is a fennel-flavored finocchiona, a salame from Tuscany. A few slices of the best mortadella, speckled with the acid green of fresh pistachio nuts, and of tasty coppa, which is a rolled, cured, and boned shoulder of pork, would be just right for a good assortment.

The prosciutto can be prosciutto di Parma, the sweetest and palest of them all, or prosciutto di San Daniele, made in Friuli, of a darker red and stronger flavor. There is also a prosciutto di Carpegna, which is available in some of the best Italian grocers. I like it because it has a good flavor, is usually perfectly salted, and contains the right amount of fat. A good prosciutto should always have some fat.

As for the quantity, I find that about 2 ounces per person is enough. However, it is probably a good idea to buy more, because if you have a few slices left over they came in very handy for a sandwich the next day.

Try to buy your salumi from a grocers where it is sliced in front of you, rather than in vacuum packs from a supermarket. It is usually a better product and you can see with your own eyes if it is really the salami it purports to be. For instance, prosciutti have a mark of origin, their D.O.C. stamped on the skin. If you ask for the salumi to be sliced, remember that prosciutto should be sliced fine, but not so fine that you cannot transfer the slice to a dish without breaking it. Salami are better thicker, and the smaller the diameter of the salame, the thicker the cut should be.

CROSTINI E BRUSCHETTA

TOASTED AND GRILLED BREAD

Although I hate to think of food as being subject to fashion, I have to accept this fact of life. In this chapter you will find recipes for the most fashionable Italian antipasti of the early '90s. To me, however, Bruschetta and Crostini are dishes I have always made and shall always make, certainly not every week but at the right time of year, when I am in Italy or when I can get hold of the perfect tomatoes or am given a white truffle, or I am in the mood to make a loaf of bread (this latter a very rare event).

Crostini cover a broader range of dishes than Bruschetta. Crostini consist of slices of toasted bread moistened with olive oil on which different toppings are spread, while Bruschetta is either grilled country bread flavored with olive oil and garlic, or the same grilled bread topped with tomato.

This antipasto has the advantage that it can be served as "finger food" with the pre-dinner drinks, thus eliminating the washing of one set of plates.

FONDUTA PIEMONTESE
PIEDMONTESE FONDUE

Serves 4

14 ounces Italian fontina cheese
1 cup & 2 tablespoons whole milk
4 tablespoons unsalted butter
4 egg yolks
1 white truffle or 1 tablespoon truffle paste

Fontina, the best-known cheese from Valle d'Aosta, used to be made at Mont Fontin, from which it takes its name. It is the main ingredient of this classic dish. The other characteristic ingredient is the white truffle of Alba. There are now various brands of truffle paste on the market, made with white truffles and porcini, which works very well in a fonduta. Sliced bread or crostini (see page 11) are served with fonduta for dipping into it. I also like to use thick slices of broiled polenta.

1 About 6 hours before you want to serve the fonduta, cut the fontina into small dice. Put in a bowl and add enough milk just to cover the cheese. Set aside.

2 Put the butter in the top of a double boiler, add the fontina with the milk, and set over simmering water.

3 Cook, stirring constantly, until the cheese has melted, about 10 minutes. Beat in the egg yolks, one at a time. Continue cooking, beating the whole time, until the egg has been absorbed and the sauce reaches the consistency of thick cream. If you are using truffle paste, mix it in at this point, off the heat.

4 Transfer the fonduta to individual soup bowls and slice the truffle over it, if you are using this food of the gods. Serve immediately.

CROSTINI ALLA TOSCANA
CHICKEN LIVER CROSTINI

In Tuscany, where this dish comes from, they add calf's spleen to the chicken liver and to give the mixture more volume. Of all variety meats, spleen is the only one that is always used with other types. To give this extra consistency to the mixture I have substituted ground beef for the calf's spleen. It works very well.

You can moisten the bread with vinsanto mixed with broth, instead of the more common olive oil. Vinsanto is a very strong wine from Chianti, made from grapes that are left to dry several weeks before they are pressed.

1 Remove the fat, gristle, and any greenish bits from the chicken livers. Wash, dry, and chop as finely as you can.

2 Put the olive oil in a saucepan and, when just hot, add the celery, shallot, garlic, and parsley. Cook until soft, about 10 minutes, stirring frequently.

3 Add the chicken livers and beef and cook over very low heat until the chicken livers have lost their raw color and have become crumbly.

4 Mix in the tomato paste and cook 1 minute. Raise the heat, pour in the wine, and boil to reduce until nearly all the wine has evaporated. Lower the heat and add a little salt and plenty of pepper. Simmer gently 30 minutes, adding a little hot water if the mixture gets too dry.

5 Mix in the capers and anchovies. Add the butter and cook gently 5 minutes, stirring constantly.

6 Spread the mixture on crostini (see page 11) moistened with olive oil or with a mixture of good beef broth and vinsanto.

Serves 6–8

$\frac{1}{2}$ pound chicken livers
$\frac{1}{4}$ cup olive oil (for cooking)
$\frac{1}{2}$ celery stalk, minced
1 shallot, minced
2 small garlic cloves, peeled and chopped
3 tablespoons chopped fresh parsley
$\frac{1}{4}$ pound lean ground beef
1 tablespoon tomato paste
6 tablespoons dry white wine
salt and freshly ground black pepper
1 tablespoon capers, rinsed and chopped
2 salted anchovies, boned and rinsed, or 4 canned anchovy fillets, chopped
2 tablespoons unsalted butter

PURE DI FAVE

FAVA BEAN PURÉE

Serves 6–8

3 pounds fresh fava beans, or
1 pound frozen lima beans
salt and freshly ground
black pepper
3 garlic cloves, peeled
2 ounces good-quality crustless
white bread
milk
6 tablespoons extra virgin
olive oil

For this recipe you can use frozen lima beans which, although they do not have all the sweet mealiness of fresh fava beans, are picked and frozen at their best. Some recipes suggest using boiled potatoes instead of the bread. Either version is good.

1 Shell the beans, if you are using fresh favas. Cook the fresh or frozen beans in a saucepan of simmering water to which you have added 1 tablespoon of salt and the peeled garlic. The beans should cook at the lowest simmer. When the beans are tender, drain them and the garlic, reserving $\frac{1}{2}$ cup of the liquid. Let cool.
2 Put the bread in a bowl and pour in enough milk just to cover the bread.
3 Now you must have the patience to slip off the white skin from the fava beans. It's rather a boring and lengthy job, but it is necessary if you want a really creamy purée without those unpleasant pieces of papery skin. If there are any children around the house enlist their help; they usually love popping the beans out of their skin.
4 Put the beans, the garlic, and bread with its milk in a food processor and whizz to a purée, while gradually adding all but about 1 tablespoon of the oil through the funnel. If the purée is very thick, add a little of the reserved bean cooking liquid. Taste and adjust the seasoning, adding a little of the reserved water if too thick.
5 You can spread the purée on crostini (see page 11) moistened with the reserved oil, or serve the purée piled up in a dish surrounded by crostini, and let your guests or family do the work.

INTINGOLO DI PEPERONI E POMODORI SECCHI
— RELISH OF BELL PEPPERS AND SUN-DRIED TOMATOES —

This colorful relish is good spooned over crostini (see page 11) or over slices of broiled polenta.

1 Put the sun-dried tomatoes in a bowl. Add enough boiling water to cover, and the vinegar. Let soak about 2 hours. Drain, reserving the liquid, and pat dry with paper towels. Cut the tomatoes into $\frac{1}{2}$-inch pieces and set aside.

2 Heat the oven to 450°F and put a small baking sheet in the oven.

3 Put the peppers on the baking sheet and bake until they are soft, about 30 minutes. Remove from the oven and let cool a little.

4 Meanwhile, heat the onion and oil in a small frying pan. Sauté a few minutes, and then add the garlic, chili pepper, and a little of the reserved tomato liquid, so that the *soffritto* (frying mixture) does not stick to the pan. Continue cooking until very soft, stirring frequently.

5 Peel the peppers, cut them in half, and discard core and seeds. Cut them into $\frac{1}{2}$-inch pieces and set aside.

6 Mix the tomato pieces into the *soffritto* in the pan, adding a little more of the tomato liquid if the mixture is dry. Cook, stirring frequently, 5 minutes or so and then add the peppers. Let the peppers *insaporire* – take up the flavor.

7 Add the anchovy fillet to the pan and squash it down to a purée. Mix in the capers. Taste and adjust the seasoning. Serve warm or cold.

Serves 4

1 ounce loose sun-dried tomatoes (not packed in oil)
2 tablespoons red wine vinegar
2 large red and/or yellow bell peppers
$\frac{1}{2}$ sweet onion, very finely chopped
2 tablespoons extra virgin olive oil
1 garlic clove, minced
$\frac{1}{2}$ dried hot chili pepper, crumbled
1 canned anchovy fillet, chopped
1 tablespoon capers, rinsed and dried
salt and freshly ground black pepper

BRUSCHETTA

ROMAN GARLIC BREAD

Bruschetta is a crisp, charred-tasting bread, originally from Rome (*bruscare* means "to burn lightly" in Roman dialect). It is made with coarse country bread, which has a high nutritional value. For centuries bruschetta has been a staple dish of the poor, who ironically used to call it *cappone* – capon – since it was the nearest they could get to his delicacy of the rich. Nowadays, bruschetta is served as an appetizer while you wait for your pasta to be ready. Bruschetta is also ideal to eat with fish soups.

Cut a loaf of coarse white bread – I use a Pugliese loaf – into really thick ($\frac{1}{2}$- to $\frac{3}{4}$-inch) slices. For 6 slices you will need 2 squashed garlic cloves, some extra virgin olive oil, preferably a peppery Tuscan oil, and a good deal of freshly ground black pepper.

Score the slices lightly with the point of a small knife in a criss-cross fashion. Grill the bread on both sides over charcoal or wood embers (or under the broiler) and then, while still hot, rub it with the garlic. Put the slices in a hot oven for 2 minutes, to make them crisp through, and then place them on a plate. Drizzle about 1 tablespoon of oil over each one and sprinkle generously with pepper and a little salt.

This is the authentic, traditional bruschetta. In the last few years bruschetta has come to mean a thick, charred slice of bread moistened with olive oil and topped with tomatoes. Here is one recipe made with sun-dried tomatoes for the winter.

BRUSCHETTA COI POMODORI SECCHI
BRUSCHETTA WITH SUN-DRIED TOMATOES

1 Reconstitute the sun-dried tomatoes at least 1 day in advance: put them in a bowl, cover them with boiling water, add the vinegar, and let soak 2 hours or so.

2 Drain the tomatoes and dry them thoroughly with paper towels. Cut them into $\frac{1}{2}$-inch strips and put the strips in a deep dish. Pour the olive oil over the tomatoes, place the garlic here and there, and add the chili pepper. Let marinate at least 24 hours.

3 Score the bread lightly with the point of a knife in a criss-cross fashion. Grill or broil the slices on both sides and then moisten them with the oil in which the tomatoes have marinated. Lay a few strips of tomato over each slice of bread, leaving the garlic and chili behind.

Serves 4–5

2 ounces loose sun-dried tomatoes (not packed in oil)
2 tablespoons wine vinegar
6 tablespoons extra virgin olive oil
3 garlic cloves, cut into large pieces
2 dried hot chili peppers, cut in half
6 slices of good-quality crusty bread

INSALATE

SALADS

Amixed antipasto for a large party, or an antipasto trolley in a restaurant, usually contains a number of different salads. Grilled bell peppers, for instance, are a classic antipasto salad, as are tomatoes with mozzarella and basil. The following five recipes include some of my favorites and some classics.

INSALATA DI PERE E FORMAGGIO
PEAR AND CHEESE SALAD

Serves 4

4 ripe Bartlett or Comice pears
$\frac{1}{4}$ pound Parmigiano Reggiano or
good padano cheese
$\frac{1}{4}$ pound aged romano cheese
3 tablespoons extra virgin
olive oil
2 tablespoons lemon juice
salt and freshly ground
black pepper
$\frac{1}{4}$ pound arugula

We have a saying in Italy, "Do not let the peasant know how good pears are with cheese" – or he might pick all the pears off your tree! This salad is a sophisticated version of the classic pears with cheese.

1 Peel the pears, cut them into quarters, and remove cores. Cut each quarter in half and pile them up in a deep dish.
2 Cut the cheeses into small cubes of about $\frac{1}{2}$-inch. Mix into the pears.
3 Beat the oil and lemon juice together and add salt and pepper to taste. Spoon about half this dressing over the pears and let marinate 1 hour.
4 Surround the pear and cheese mound with arugula and drizzle the rest of the dressing over it. Serve immediately.

INSALATA DI BROCCOLI CON LA MOLLICA

BROCCOLI AND BREAD CRUMB SALAD

Brown bread crumbs are better than white for this tasty dish from southern Italy. I make my fresh crumbs in a food processor, a very quick job. You can use cauliflower instead of broccoli.

1 Divide the broccoli into small florets. Peel the outer layer from the stems and cut them into small pieces. Blanch the florets and pieces of stem in boiling salted water until just tender, about 5 minutes. Drain and dry with paper towels. Transfer to a bowl add 2 tablespoons of the oil. Toss gently, using two forks, rather than spoons, as they are less likely to break the florets.

2 Heat the rest of the oil in a frying pan and add the bread crumbs. Cook 3 minutes, stirring to coat them with the oil.

3 Chop all the other ingredients, except the olives, and add them to the bread mixture. Add the olives and cook another minute or so, stirring well. Taste and add salt and pepper as necessary.

4 Toss half the bread-crumb mixture into the broccoli and spoon the rest over the top. Serve warm.

Serves 4

1 pound broccoli
6 tablespoons extra virgin olive oil
$2\frac{2}{3}$ cups fresh bread crumbs
6 canned anchovy fillets, drained, or 3 salted anchovies, boned and rinsed
1 or 2 dried hot chili peppers, according to taste, seeded
2 garlic cloves, peeled
$1\frac{1}{4}$ tablespoons capers, rinsed and dried
12 black olives, pitted and cut into strips
salt and freshly ground black pepper

PEPERONI ARROSTITI

GRILLED BELL PEPPERS

Serves 4

4 beautiful red or yellow
bell peppers
6 canned anchovy fillets,
drained, or 3 salted anchovies,
boned and rinsed
3 garlic cloves
2 tablespoons chopped
fresh parsley
1 small dried hot chili pepper,
seeded
$\frac{1}{4}$ cup extra virgin olive oil

When bell peppers are grilled and skinned their taste is totally different from that of raw or sautéed peppers. To my mind they are much nicer, and they are certainly more digestible. You can prepare a few pounds of peppers when they are in season, and reasonably cheap, and keep them in the refrigerator in jars, well covered with olive oil, for 2 or 3 months.

When I serve these peppers on their own I like to dress them with the sauce given below, which is based on olive oil and garlic to which anchovy fillets and capers can be added. The sauce should be cooked a couple of minutes so that the garlic and anchovy flavor combines well and becomes less pervasive. However, it is very important that the sauce should cook over very low heat or the garlic will burn and the anchovy will become bitter.

1 Hold the peppers over the flame of a burner or set them in hot charcoal and grill them all over. (Alternatively, put them under the broiler.) When the side in contact with the heat is charred, turn the pepper, until all the surface, including the top and bottom, is charred. As soon as all the skin is charred, take the pepper from the heat, otherwise the flesh will begin to burn and you will be left with paper-thin peppers.
2 Let the peppers cool and then remove the skin; it will come off very easily as long as the peppers have been well charred. Cut the peppers in half, remove the stem and seeds, and then cut them lengthwise into strips. Put them in a shallow dish.
3 Pound the anchovies with the garlic, parsley, and chili pepper in a mortar, or chop very finely.

4 Put the oil and the anchovy mixture in a heavy-bottomed pan and heat very slowly, stirring and pounding the whole time until the mixture is mashed. Spoon the anchovy mixture over the peppers and let marinate at least 4 hours. The longer you leave them – up to a week – the better they get. Serve plenty of bread with them.

POMODORI CON LA MOZZARELLA
E IL BASILICO

—————— TOMATOES, MOZZARELLA, AND BASIL ——————

Serves 4

12 ripe tomatoes
salt and freshly ground
black pepper
$\frac{3}{4}$ pound buffalo mozzarella
cheese
6 tablespoons extra virgin
olive oil
24 fresh basil leaves

This is the simplest and best summer antipasto. However, do not make it unless you have very good tomatoes – tasty and juicy, not woolly and dry. Sometimes you can buy the best round tomatoes from Calabria or Campania, sold still attached to their branches. Also, use buffalo mozzarella, which has a much deeper flavor than cows'-milk mozzarella.

This might, in fact, be the sort of dish you can best prepare during your Mediterranean vacation, when you are sure of being able to buy the perfect ingredients.

1 The tomatoes must be peeled without being blanched, as this would soften them. To do this, use a swivel-bladed vegetable peeler. Make a small incision at one end of the tomato and start from there, working with the peeler by pushing it lightly backward and forward in a sawing movement. It is quite easy once you have learned the knack, which applies also to peeling raw bell peppers.
2 When all the tomatoes are peeled, cut them in half. Squeeze out a little of the seeds and juice, and then sprinkle with salt. Lay the tomato halves on a wooden board, cut-side down. Put the board in the refrigerator and leave at least 30 minutes.
3 Wipe the inside of the tomatoes with paper towels and place them, cut-side up, on a platter.
4 Cut the mozzarella into 24 slices or pieces. Put 1 piece inside each tomato half. Season with a generous grinding of pepper and drizzle with the olive oil.
5 Wipe the basil leaves with a moistened piece of paper towel. Place a leaf over each piece of mozzarella.

PANZANELLA
BREAD AND RAW VEGETABLE SALAD

A traditional rustic salad made in the summer with country bread and seasonal raw vegetables. Make it only when good tomatoes are in season, and with country-type bread. I recommend a Pugliese loaf, available in some supermarkets or in good Italian grocers.

1 Cover the bread with cold water to which you have added 1 tablespoon of the vinegar. Let soak until just soft, then squeeze out all the liquid and put the bread in a salad bowl. The bread should be damp but not wet. Break it up with a fork.

2 Add the basil, garlic, cucumber, onion, and tomatoes. Season with salt and pepper. Toss thoroughly with the oil, using a fork to turn the mixture over. Chill 30 minutes or so.

3 Taste and add more vinegar to your liking. It is not possible to specify the amount of vinegar, since it depends on its acidity and on personal taste.

Serves 4

8 slices of good-quality white bread, 1 day old
about 2 tablespoons wine vinegar
12 fresh basil leaves, coarsely torn
$\frac{1}{2}$ garlic clove, minced
1 cucumber, peeled and cut into $\frac{1}{2}$-inch slices
$\frac{1}{2}$ red onion, very thinly sliced
$\frac{1}{2}$ pound ripe meaty tomatoes, seeded and cut into $\frac{1}{2}$-inch cubes
salt and freshly ground black pepper
6 tablespoons extra virgin olive oil

VERDURE RIPIENE

One of the joys of walking around the old part of Genova is that you can still see shops selling arinata (chickpea tart), focaccia, pissaladeira, and stuffed vegetables, all in the huge, round copper pans in which they have been baked. Fat red tomatoes and shimmering red and yellow bell peppers fight for space with eggplants, of all colors from purple to ivory, and plump round zucchini, all soft and glistening with oil.

The recipes that follow are for my favorite stuffed vegetables. If you choose two or three of them and serve them together, you are sure to give your family and friends one of the most appetizing and satisfying antipasti ever.

The tomatoes, bell peppers, and zucchini, for instance, go together very well, while the eggplants are perfect also by themselves. All these stuffed vegetables are best served warm or at room temperature, but not hot or chilled. They are even more delicious if made a day in advance.

FUNGHETTI RIPIENI ALLA GENOVESE

STUFFED MUSHROOM CAPS

Serves 4

$\frac{3}{4}$ ounce dried porcini
1 pound large-cap mushrooms
1 cup fresh white bread crumbs
1 salted anchovy, boned and
rinsed, or 2 canned
anchovy fillets
1 or 2 garlic cloves, according
to taste, peeled
a handful of fresh marjoram
pinch of grated nutmeg
salt and freshly ground
black pepper
$\frac{1}{4}$ cup extra virgin olive oil
2 tablespoons chopped fresh
flat-leaf Italian parsley

If you can find them, use fresh porcini (cèpes). Otherwise you can use cultivated large mushrooms, plus a little dried porcini for better flavor, as in this recipe.

1 Soak the dried porcini in very hot water for 30 minutes. Drain and, if necessary, rinse under cold water to remove any trace of grit. Dry thoroughly with paper towels.

2 Gently wipe the large-cap mushrooms with a damp cloth and detach the stems.

3 Chop together the dried porcini, mushroom stems, bread crumbs, anchovies, garlic, and marjoram. You can use a food processor, but do not reduce to pulp. Transfer to a bowl and add the nutmeg and salt and pepper to taste.

4 Heat the oven to 425°F.

5 Heat 2 tablespoons of the oil in a frying pan and add the mushroom and bread crumb mixture. Sauté 5 minutes, stirring frequently.

6 Lay the mushroom caps on an oiled baking sheet, hollow-side up. Sprinkle them with salt and then fill them with the crumb mixture. Sprinkle a pinch or two of parsley on top of each cap and then drizzle with the remaining oil. Bake until the caps are soft, 10–15 minutes. Serve at room temperature.

POMODORI AMMOLLICATI

TOMATOES STUFFED WITH BREAD CRUMBS
AND PARSLEY

1 Cut the tomatoes in half. Remove the seeds and sprinkle with salt. Lay them cut-side down on a wooden board to drain about 30 minutes. Wipe the inside of each half with paper towels.

2 Heat the oven to 350°F

3 Put the parsley, garlic, capers, chili pepper, bread crumbs, and oregano in a bowl. Mix well and then add 4 tablespoons of the oil. Season with a little salt and some pepper. Mix well to a paste.

4 Oil the bottom of a shallow baking dish or roasting pan. Place the tomatoes in the dish, cut-side up.

5 Spoon a little of the bread-crumb mixture into each tomato half and then drizzle with the rest of the oil. Bake until the tomatoes are soft but still whole, about 30 minutes. Serve at room temperature.

Serves 3 or 4

6 large round tomatoes, ripe but firm
salt and freshly ground black pepper
2 tablespoons chopped fresh flat-leaf Italian parsley
2 garlic cloves, minced
1 tablespoon capers, rinsed and chopped
$\frac{1}{2}$ small dried hot chili pepper, chopped
$\frac{1}{4}$ cup dry white bread crumbs
$\frac{1}{2}$ tablespoon dried oregano
$\frac{1}{3}$ cup extra virgin olive oil

MELANZANE RIPIENE

EGGPLANT STUFFED WITH SAUSAGE, PINE NUTS, AND CURRANTS

Serves 4

2 eggplants, weighing about
1 pound each
salt and freshly ground
black pepper
4 tablespoons extra virgin
olive oil
1 large garlic clove, minced
$\frac{1}{2}$ small onion or 1 shallot, minced
$\frac{1}{2}$ celery stalk, minced
$\frac{1}{2}$ pound spicy luganega or other
spicy coarse-grained pure pork
continental sausage, skinned
and crumbled
$\frac{2}{3}$ cup fresh white bread crumbs
3 tablespoons pine nuts
2 tablespoons capers,
rinsed and dried
1 egg
1 tablespoon dried oregano
3 tablespoons freshly grated
aged romano or Parmesan
cheese
3 tablespoons dried currants
1 large, ripe tomato

1 Wash and dry the eggplants. Cut them in half lengthwise and scoop out all the flesh with the help of a small sharp knife and then with a small teaspoon, leaving just enough pulp to cover the skin. Be careful not to pierce the skin.

2 Chop the eggplant pulp coarsely and place in a colander. Sprinkle with salt, mix well, and let drain about 1 hour.

3 Put 3 tablespoons of the oil, the garlic, the onion, and celery in a frying pan and sauté over low heat until soft, stirring frequently. Add the sausage and cook 20 minutes, turning it over frequently.

4 Meanwhile, squeeze the liquid from the chopped eggplant pulp and dry thoroughly with paper towels. Add the eggplant pulp to the pan and fry gently a few minutes, stirring frequently. Taste and adjust the seasoning.

5 Heat the oven to 375°F.

6 Add the bread crumbs to the mixture in the frying pan. After 2–3 minutes, mix in the pine nuts. Cook a further 30 seconds, then transfer to a bowl.

7 Add the capers, egg, oregano, cheese, currants, and pepper to taste to the mixture in the bowl and mix very thoroughly. Taste and add salt if necessary.

8 Pat dry the inside of the eggplant shells. Oil a baking dish large enough to hold the eggplant shells in a single layer. Place the eggplant shells, one next to the other, in the ovenproof dish and fill them with the sausage mixture.

9 Cut the tomato into strips and place 2 or 3 strips on the top of each eggplant half. Drizzle with the rest of the oil. Add $\frac{1}{2}$ cup of water to the bottom of the dish. Cover the dish tightly with foil and bake 20 minutes. Remove the foil and bake 20 minutes more.

This dish is best eaten warm, an hour or so after it comes out of the oven.

PEPERONI AMMOLLICATI
BELL PEPPERS STUFFED WITH BREAD CRUMBS
AND PARSLEY

Serves 4

1½ pounds red and yellow
bell peppers
⅓ cup extra virgin olive oil
salt and freshly ground
black pepper
3 tablespoons chopped fresh
flat-leaf Italian parsley
2 garlic cloves, minced
1 tablespoon capers, rinsed and
chopped
½ small dried hot chili pepper,
chopped
2 salted anchovies, boned,
rinsed, and chopped
¼ cup dry white bread crumbs

The stuffing for bell peppers is basically the same as that for tomatoes. I prefer, however, to omit the oregano and to add salted anchovies. Use red and yellow peppers, but not green because they are not sweet enough.

1 Cut the peppers into quarters and remove the cores, ribs, and seeds. Heat 4 tablespoons of the oil in a large frying pan until very hot and then add the peppers, skin-side down. Sprinkle with salt and pepper and cook about 10 minutes, shaking the pan occasionally.

2 Heat the oven to 350°F.

3 Mix together the remaining ingredients in a bowl.

4 When the peppers are just soft, place them in an oiled baking dish, cut-side up. Pour the juices from the pan into the bread-crumb mixture and mix well. Taste and check seasoning.

5 Place a small mound of stuffing into each piece of pepper, drizzle with the remaining oil, and bake 15 minutes.

ZUCCHINE AL FORNO

BAKED ZUCCHINI WITH MINT

AND GARLIC STUFFING

1 Cut the zucchini in half lengthwise. Make some diagonal incisions on the cut side. Sprinkle the cut side lightly with salt and place the zucchini halves on a wooden board, cut-side down. This will let some of the liquid to drain away.

2 Heat the oven to 350°F.

3 Put the chopped herbs in a bowl and add the garlic and the bread crumbs. Add half the oil gradually, while beating with a fork. Season with a good grinding of pepper and with very little salt.

4 Oil a shallow baking dish or a lasagna dish large enough to hold all the zucchini halves in a single layer.

5 Wipe the zucchini with paper towels and lay them in the dish, cut-side up. Spoon a little of the herb mixture over each half. Drizzle 1 tablespoon of the oil over the halves and cover the dish with foil. Bake 15 minutes. Remove the foil and continue baking until the zucchini are tender and the top is crisp, about 10 minutes more.

6 Drizzle with the remaining oil while the zucchini are still hot. Serve warm or at room temperature.

Serves 4

1 pound medium zucchini
salt and freshly ground
black pepper
2 tablespoons chopped
fresh parsley
$\frac{1}{4}$ cup chopped fresh mint
2 garlic cloves, chopped
$\frac{1}{4}$ cup dry bread crumbs
6 tablespoons extra virgin
olive oil

ANTIPASTI DI PESCE E CARNE

The following recipes are for dishes whose main ingredient, whether fish or meat, is usually served as a main course. In these recipes the fish and meat is prepared in a light and lively way that is extremely appetizing and therefore particularly suited to antipasto.

COZZE RIPIENE

STUFFED MUSSELS

Serves 4

2 pounds mussels
2 unwaxed lemons, cut into quarters
6 garlic cloves, peeled
$\frac{1}{2}$ cup extra virgin olive oil
$\frac{1}{3}$ cup chopped fresh parsley
$\frac{1}{3}$ cup dry bread crumbs
salt and freshly ground black pepper

This is the basic recipe for cozze ripiene, to which other ingredients such as grated romano cheese, tomato sauce, capers, and so on can be added.

1 Mussels are much cleaner these days, because they are usually farmed. However, they still need a good cleaning. Put them in a sink full of cold water and scrub them with a stiff brush. Scrape off any barnacles and beards. Discard any mussel that stays open after tapping it against a hard surface: it is dead. Rinse the mussels in several changes of water until the water is clean and no sand is left at the bottom of the sink.

2 Put the lemon quarters and 5 cloves of garlic in a large frying pan. Add the mussels, cover, and cook over high heat until the mussels are open. (Discard any that remain closed. They might be full of sand.) Shake the pan occasionally.

3 Heat the oven to 425°F.

4 Remove the top of each shell. Loosen the mussels in the bottom shell and place them on a baking sheet.

5 Filter the mussel liquid left in the pan through a strainer lined with cheesecloth into a bowl. Mix in the oil, parsley, bread crumbs, and salt and pepper to taste. Mince the remaining garlic and add to the mixture.

6 Place a little of the parsley and bread crumb mixture on each mussel. Bake until golden brown, about 7 minutes.

INSALATA CALDA DI MARE

WARM SEAFOOD SALAD

This is a very popular antipasto, and every region, every town, even every cook has a slightly different version. You can vary the fish you use, according to your taste and the availability of the fish in the market. Remember to have a good selection of textures, but do not use any kind of oily fish, as its taste would be too strong.

Here is my seafood salad, which I like to serve warm.

Serves 6

1 pound mussels
1 dried hot chili pepper
1 pound squid
$\frac{1}{4}$ cup wine vinegar
1 onion, cut in half
2 bay leaves
salt and freshly ground
black pepper
$\frac{3}{4}$ pound monkfish
$\frac{1}{2}$ pound sea scallops
12 large raw shrimp in shell,
about $\frac{1}{2}$ pound
1 garlic clove, minced
3 tablespoons chopped fresh
flat-leaf Italian parsley
3 tablespoons lemon juice
$\frac{2}{3}$ cup extra virgin olive oil
black olives for garnish

1 Put the mussels in a sink full of cold water and scrub them with a stiff brush, scraping off any barnacles and beards with a small knife. Discard any open mussel that fails to close after being tapped hard on a hard surface. Rinse the mussels in several changes of water until the water is clean and no sand is left at the bottom of the sink.

2 Put the mussels in a large saucepan, cover and cook over high heat until they are open, shaking the pan every now and then. (Discard any mussels that remain closed.) Shell the mussels and put the meat in a bowl; discard the shells. Filter the mussel liquid left in the pan through a strainer lined with cheesecloth. Pour the liquid over the mussels. Add the chili pepper for flavoring.

3 Ask your fish merchant to clean and skin the squid. If he is not prepared to do it, proceed as follows: Hold the sac in one hand and pull off the tentacles with the other hand. The contents of the sac will come out, too. Cut the tentacles above the eyes. Squeeze out the thin bony beak in the center of the tentacles. Peel off the skin from the sac and the flap. Remove the translucent backbone from inside the sac and rinse the sac and tentacles under cold water. Cut the sac into strips and the tentacles into bite-size pieces.

4 Put about $1\frac{1}{2}$ quarts of cold water in a saucepan, add 2 table-spoons of the vinegar, the onion, 1 bay leaf, and some salt, and bring to a boil. Add the squid and cook at a steady simmer for 5–15 minutes, depending on their size. Squid are cooked when they become white and lose their translucency and you can pierce them with a fork. Remove the squid from the water with a slotted spoon, drain well, and add to the mussels in the bowl.

5 Cut the monkfish into large chunks and add to the boiling water in which the squid cooked. Simmer gently about 2 minutes. Remove from the heat, leaving the fish in the liquid.

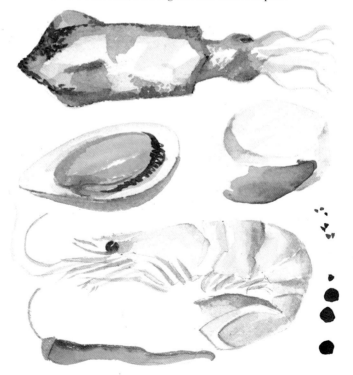

6 While the monkfish is cooking, put another saucepan on the heat with $2\frac{1}{2}$ cups of hot water, the remaining bay leaf, the rest of the vinegar, and add some salt. When the water is boiling, add the scallops. Simmer 2 minutes after the water has returned to a boil and then remove with a slotted spoon. If the scallops are large, cut them into quarters. Add to the bowl containing the mussels and the squid.

7 Put the shrimp into the same boiling water in which the scallops cooked. Simmer 1 minute after the water has come back to a boil. Drain and let to cool.

8 Drain the monkfish. Remove any bone and skin and cut into bite-size pieces. Add the fish to the bowl with the other seafood.

9 Peel the shrimp and, if necessary, devein them. Choose about 6 of the largest shrimp and set aside for garnish. Cut the other shrimp into rounds and add to the bowl.

10 Prepare the sauce: Mix the garlic, parsley, and lemon juice together in a small bowl. Add a generous grinding of black pepper and some salt. Beat in the oil slowly. Taste and adjust seasonings.

11 Before serving, put the bowl containing the seafood over a saucepan of simmering water. Cover the bowl and heat until the fish is warm, not hot. Stir it once or twice, using a fork, not a spoon, which would tend to break the pieces of fish.

12 Remove the chili and discard it. Spoon the sauce over the seafood and toss gently but thoroughly. Pile the seafood salad in a deep dish and garnish with the shrimp and the olives.

Magroni di Anatra all'Aceto Balsamico sul Letto di Valerianella

DUCK BREASTS WITH BALSAMIC VINEGAR ON A
BED OF LAMB'S LETTUCE

Serves 6

2 duck breast halves, about
$\frac{3}{4}$ pound each
salt and freshly ground
black pepper
2–3 tablespoons balsamic
vinegar, according to taste and
acidity
$\frac{1}{2}$ pound lamb's lettuce (mâche)
3 tablespoons extra virgin
olive oil

French duck breasts, called magrets de canard, are now on the market; these are the breasts of the larger but leaner Barbary ducks. These breasts have less fat under the skin, and they are ideal for this type of quick cooking. Balsamic vinegar is a superb condiment for duck. The sauce it produces when mixed with the cooking juices is rich in flavor and yet tangy enough to cut across the richness of the meat. The lamb's lettuce adds lemony crispness and a fresh look. If you cannot find lamb's lettuce, use curly endive, cut into thin strips.

1 Score the skin of the duck breast halves with the point of a small, sharp knife. Rub with salt and pepper.

2 Heat a frying pan. Place the breasts in the pan, skin-side down, and cook over medium heat 7–9 minutes, depending on thickness. The fat will be rendered. Pour nearly all the fat from the pan (keep it for sauté potatoes).

3 Spoon 1 tablespoon of balsamic vinegar over the breasts and turn them over. Cook 2 minutes on the other side. Lift out the breasts and place on a board. Carve across into $\frac{1}{4}$-inch slices. Place the slices on a warm dish. Cover with foil and set aside for 10 minutes, to let the muscle relax.

4 Add the remaining balsamic vinegar and $\frac{1}{4}$ cup of hot water to the frying pan and stir well to deglaze the juices. Taste to see if you need a little more vinegar and/or a little more water.

5 Toss the lamb's lettuce with the oil and season with a little salt and a generous grinding of pepper. Make a bed of lamb's lettuce on each plate.

6 Place the duck slices on the lamb's lettuce and pour the juices from the pan on top. Do not wait too long to serve the dish after you have poured the juices or the lettuce will "tire" too much.

SARDE A BECCAFICU
STUFFED SARDINES

The combination of sardines and orange is to be found only in Sicily, and this dish produces the best of this unusual yet delicious mixture of flavors. It is an antipasto that is very popular in Palermo and Messina, a peasant dish whose name derives from its appearance. The boned sardines are rolled up around a spoonful of stuffing and set in a dish with their tails in the air, making them look like fat little *beccafichi* – warblers – pecking at the dish.

1 Few fish merchants are willing to prepare the sardines for you, so this is what you should do: Cut off the heads and the fins (but not the tail), slit the belly, and clean out the insides. Lay the sardines on a board, open-side down, and press the backbone down gently. Cut the backbone at the tail end and remove it. Wash and dry the fish.

2 Put the currants in a bowl and cover with boiling water. Let them plump up 5–10 minutes. Drain and dry them thoroughly with paper towels.

3 Heat 3 tablespoons of the oil in a frying pan and fry the bread crumbs until nicely brown. Mix in the pine nuts, garlic, parsley,

Serves 6

2 pounds fresh sardines
$\frac{1}{4}$ cup dried currants
$\frac{1}{3}$ cup olive oil
$\frac{3}{4}$ cup dry white bread crumbs
$\frac{1}{4}$ cup pine nuts
1 garlic clove, minced
2 tablespoons chopped fresh flat-leaf Italian parsley
2 tablespoons grated aged romano cheese.
salt and freshly ground black pepper
12 dozen bay leaves
juice of 1 orange
juice of $\frac{1}{2}$ lemon
1 teaspoon sugar

and currants. Sauté gently a few minutes and then remove the pan from the heat. Add the cheese and the pepper to taste. Taste and add salt if necessary.

4 Heat the oven to 350°F.

5 Sprinkle the sardines on both sides with a little salt and pepper and place them skin-side down. Spread a heaped teaspoonful of stuffing over each fish and roll up toward the tail. Place them in an oiled baking dish with the tails sticking up in the air.

6 Stick the bay leaves here and there among the little bundles. Drizzle the orange and lemon juices and the rest of the oil all over. Sprinkle with the sugar.

7 Place the dish in the oven and bake about 15 minutes. Serve at room temperature.

SFOGI IN SAOR

SOLE FILLETS IN A SWEET-AND-SOUR
SAUCE

Serves 6–8

flour, to coat the fish
salt, to season the fish
oil for deep frying
1½ pounds sole fillets
⅓ cup golden raisins
2 tablespoons olive oil
½ pound sweet onions,
thinly sliced
2 teaspoons sugar
½ cup good wine vinegar
4 bay leaves
⅔ cup pine nuts
⅛ teaspoon ground cinnamon
2 whole cloves
12 black peppercorns,
lightly bruised

The taste of this sauce, in which the sole is marinated 2 days, is strongly reminiscent of Middle-Eastern cooking. This is understandable, as this is a dish from Venice, a city that in the past had important trade links with the Orient.

Sfogi in saor (Venetian dialect for "*sogliole in sapore*," meaning sole in a sauce) is one of the dishes traditionally eaten in Venice during the Feast of the Redeemer, which falls on the third Sunday in July, when the lagoon is lit by thousands of fireworks and carpeted with boats of every size.

1 Spread some flour on a board and season with salt.

2 Heat oil for deep frying in a wok or a frying pan. Meanwhile, coat the fish lightly in the flour.

3 When the oil is very hot but not smoking (test by frying a small piece of bread: it should brown in 50 seconds), slide in the sole fillets, a few at a time. Fry gently until a golden crust has formed, about 3 minutes on each side. With a slotted spatula, transfer the fish to a plate lined with paper towels to drain.

4 Soak the raisins in a little warm water to plump them.

5 Heat the olive oil and the onions in a small frying pan. Add a pinch of salt and the sugar. Cook the onions gently, stirring frequently, until golden. Turn the heat up and pour in the wine vinegar. Boil briskly until the liquid is reduced by half.

6 Lay the fish fillets neatly in a shallow dish. Pour the onion sauce over them and put the bay leaves on top. Drain the raisins and scatter them on top of the dish together with the pine nuts, and spices, and peppercorns. Cover the dish with plastic wrap and let marinate 24 hours.

If you want to keep the dish 2 days or more, refrigerate it. Take the dish out of the refrigerator at least 2 or 3 hours before you want to serve it, so that it has time to reach room temperature.

IL MIO CARPACCIO
MY CARPACCIO

Created by Giuseppe Cipriani at Harry's Bar for one of his clients who was on a strict diet, Carpaccio has now become the byword for any fish or meat (alas, even chicken) served raw and dressed with some sort of olive-oil-based sauce. Each cook varies the sauce according to his or her preference, so you can experiment with your Carpaccio. This is my version.

I have found it very difficult to slice the beef thinly without an electric carving knife.

Serves 4

$\frac{3}{4}$ pound beef tenderloin
1 egg yolk
$\frac{3}{4}$ cup extra virgin olive oil
3 tablespoons lemon juice
1 teaspoon Dijon mustard
a few drops of hot pepper sauce
salt and freshly ground
black pepper

1 Freeze the beef about 3 hours to harden it; this makes it easier to slice thinly.
2 Put the egg yolk in a food processor with 2 tablespoons of the oil, the lemon juice, mustard, pepper sauce, and some salt and pepper and process 30 seconds.
3 Add the rest of the oil slowly through the hole in the lid. The sauce will become like a thin mayonnaise. Taste and adjust the seasoning.
4 Remove the beef from the freezer and place it on a board. Using an electric carving knife, or a *very* sharp knife, slice it very thinly. Let the meat come back to room temperature – about 1 hour.
5 Place the meat neatly on a platter and pour the sauce over it before serving.

OTHER FAVORITES

The title of this section is self-explanatory. These are recipes I wanted to include, but which did not fit into any of the other categories.

RADICCHIO ROSSO E CICORIA BELGA ALLA TREVISANA

BROILED RADICCHIO AND BELGIAN ENDIVE

Serves 6

1 pound red radicchio
$\frac{1}{2}$ pound Belgian endive
6 tablespoons extra virgin olive oil
salt and freshly ground black pepper

The radicchio rosso used in Veneto for this dish is the long radicchio of Treviso, which can now sometimes be found in specialist stores during the fall. It has the characteristic bitterness of radicchio, delicate yet more pronounced than the round Rosa di Chioggia, which is the kind of radicchio available everywhere all year around. The Rosa di Chioggia is a modern type of radicchio which is grown in greenhouses. It is tougher in texture and blander in flavor, with a similarity to white cabbage. However, the use of heat in this recipe brings out the flavor. Belgian Endive is very good prepared in this way.

1 Preheat the broiler.

2 Wash the radicchio and the endive carefully. Dry thoroughly. Cut the heads of radicchio into quarters and the endive heads in half, both lengthwise.

3 Place the radicchio and endive in the broiler pan (or on a hot cast-iron grill pan). Spoon over the oil and season with salt and a generous amount of pepper.

4 Cook under the broiler or on the grill pan for 10 minutes, taking care to turn the heat down if the vegetables start to burn. Turn the pieces over halfway through the cooking. The vegetables are ready when the thick core can be pierced easily.

5 Transfer the vegetables to a dish and spoon over the juices from the broiler pan. Serve hot or cold.

CIPOLLINE BRASATE
BRAISED BABY ONIONS

These onions, served cold, often form part of a spectacular Piedmontese antipasto. They can also accompany cold meat or, served hot, boiled or braised meat dishes. The onions used in Italy are the white, squat kind, very sweet in taste. Unfortunately they are not easily available outside Italy, but you can use small young pearl onions instead.

1 Put the onions in a pan of boiling water. Bring back to a boil and blanch 1 minute. Drain and remove the outside skin, taking care to remove only the dangling roots and not the base of the root, otherwise the onions will come apart during the cooking.

2 Choose a large sauté pan and put in the onions, olive oil, and butter. Sauté the onions until golden, shaking the pan often.

3 Add the diluted tomato paste, sugar, vinegar and salt and pepper to taste. Cook, uncovered, about 1 hour, adding a little more water if necessary. The onions are ready when they are a rich brown color and can easily be pierced by a fork. Serve hot or cold, but not chilled.

Serves 4

$1\frac{1}{2}$ pounds small onions
$\frac{1}{4}$ cup olive oil
1 tablespoon butter
2 teaspoons tomato paste
dissolved in $\frac{2}{3}$ cup hot water
2 tablespoons sugar
2 tablespoons red wine vinegar
salt and freshly ground
black pepper

FRITTELLE DI MOZZARELLA

MOZZARELLA AND PARMESAN FRITTERS

Serves 4

$\frac{1}{2}$ pound Italian mozzarella cheese
1 extra large egg
$\frac{3}{4}$ cup freshly grated Parmesan cheese
2 tablespoons flour
12 fresh basil leaves
1 small garlic clove, minced
salt and freshly ground black pepper
oil for deep frying
dish

The mozzarella must be left out of its pack for 24 hours to allow it to dry out.

1 Shred the mozzarella through the largest holes of a cheese grater and put it in a bowl.
2 Beat the egg lightly and add to the bowl with the Parmesan and flour.
3 Wipe the basil leaves with damp paper towels and snip them with scissors. Mix into the mozzarella mixture with the garlic, a generous grinding of pepper, and a little salt. (Add the salt with caution because the Parmesan is salty.) Mix thoroughly.
4 With damp hands, shape the mixture into small balls, the size of a walnut. If the mixture is too sloppy, add a little more flour. Put the balls on a wooden board and chill at least 30 minutes.
5 Heat oil in a wok or a deep saucepan. When the oil is very hot but not yet smoking (the right temperature is 350°F, i.e. when a small piece of bread will turn golden in 50 seconds) slide in the cheese balls. Do not crowd the pan or they will not fry properly. Turn them over and when they are deep gold all over, remove them with a slotted spoon and put them on paper towels to drain. Serve hot.

CAROTE IN AGRODOLCE
CARROTS IN A WINE AND HERB
SAUCE

Vegetables these days badly need an uplift. This agrodolce treatment is just the thing to bring out the delicious sweet taste of the carrots.

Serves 6

2 pounds carrots
6 tablespoons olive oil
1 cup dry white wine
$\frac{1}{2}$ cup white wine vinegar
2 sprigs of fresh flat-leaf
Italian parsley
2 sprigs of fresh thyme
4 fresh sage leaves
2 bay leaves
4 sprigs of fresh mint
2 garlic cloves, cut in half
salt and freshly ground
black pepper
2 tablespoons sugar

1 Cut the carrots into thick matchsticks and put them in a sauté pan.

2 Add all the other ingredients plus 1 cup of water. Bring to a boil and cook, uncovered, 30 minutes. The carrots will still be quite crunchy.

3 Lift the carrots out of the pan with a slotted spoon and put them in a bowl.

4 Boil the liquid rapidly to reduce until it is very tasty and of a beautiful deep gold color. Most of the water will have evaporated and you will be left with a delicious hot herby vinaigrette. Taste and adjust the seasoning.

5 Pour the reduced liquid over the carrots and let marinate 48 hours.

6 Remove the herbs and garlic before serving.

Uova Soda alla Pugliese con i Pomodori Secchi

Hard-Boiled Eggs with Parsley and Bread Crumb Topping and Sun-Dried Tomatoes

Serves 4

¼ pound loose sun-dried tomatoes (not packed in oil)
6 tablespoons good red wine vinegar, but not balsamic vinegar
⅔ cup extra virgin olive oil
salt and freshly ground black pepper
6 eggs
6 tablespoons dry white bread crumbs
3 garlic cloves, chopped
6 tablespoons chopped fresh flat-leaf Italian parsley
2–3 dried hot chili peppers, according to taste, chopped

These eggs are served at room temperature. I like to surround them with charred and peeled yellow and red bell peppers (page 22), or, as here, with sun-dried tomatoes generously dressed with extra virgin olive oil and seasoned with garlic, salt, and pepper. I also scatter black olives here and there around the dish.

1 Put the sun-dried tomatoes in a bowl and cover with boiling water. Add 4 tablespoons of the vinegar and let soak about 2 hours. Lift the tomatoes out of the liquid and pat dry thoroughly with paper towels. Drizzle 2 tablespoons of the oil over the tomatoes and season with salt and pepper. Set aside while you prepare the eggs.

2 Hard boil the eggs: Lower them into a pan of simmering water and boil 8 minutes, no longer, so that the yolks will be just hard. Put the saucepan under cold running water and leave 1 minute. Crack the shells all around and peel them off. Let the eggs cool completely in the cold water while you make the topping.

3 Heat half the remaining oil in a small frying pan. Add the bread crumbs and sauté, stirring constantly, until the crumbs are golden, 3–4 minutes. Put aside 2–3 tablespoons of the remaining oil. Add the rest of the oil to the pan with the remaining vinegar and all the other ingredients. Sauté gently 3–4 minutes more. Taste and adjust the seasoning.

4 Drain and dry the eggs. Cut them in half lengthwise. To prevent the egg halves sliding on the dish, slice off a tiny bit of the white on the round side, to give a flat base. Arrange the eggs on a

serving dish and drizzle with the reserved oil. Season lightly with salt and pepper and pile about 2 teaspoons of the topping over each egg half. Surround with the tomatoes.

CAPONATA

EGGPLANT, ONION, AND CELERY STEW

Thanks to the creativity of the Sicilians, the humble eggplant here forms the basis of one of the grandest vegetable dishes. Caponata appears in many different versions throughout the island. The dish can be garnished with tiny boiled octopus, with a small lobster, with shrimp, or with *bottarga* – the dried roe of the gray mullet or of the tuna fish, a specialty of Sicily and Sardinia. I garnish this one with hard-boiled eggs, thus making it a perfect vegetarian dish.

The secret of a good caponata is that the three vegetables – eggplant, celery, and onion – must be cooked separately and only after cooking combined together and added to the other ingredients. Caponata is best made at least 24 hours in advance.

1 Cut the eggplants into $\frac{1}{2}$-inch cubes.

2 Heat 1 inch of vegetable oil in a frying pan. When the oil is hot (it is ready when it sizzles around a cube of eggplant) add a layer of eggplant cubes and fry until golden brown on all sides. Drain on paper towels. Repeat until all the eggplant cubes are cooked. Season each batch lightly with salt.

3 Cut the celery into pieces of the same size as the eggplant. Fry it in the oil in which you fried the eggplant, until golden and crisp. Drain it on paper towels.

Serves 4

$1\frac{1}{2}$ pound eggplants
vegetable oil for frying
salt and freshly ground
black pepper
the inner sticks of 1 bunch of
celery, coarse threads
removed.
$\frac{1}{2}$ cup olive oil
1 onion, very finely sliced
1 cup canned Italian plum
tomatoes, chopped
1 tablespoon sugar
6 tablespoons white
wine vinegar
1 tablespoon grated semisweet
chocolate
$\frac{1}{3}$ cup capers
$\frac{1}{3}$ cup large green olives, pitted
and quartered
2 hard-boiled eggs

4 Pour the olive oil into a clean frying pan and add the onion. Sauté gently until soft, about 10 minutes. Add the tomatoes and cook, stirring frequently, over medium heat about 15 minutes. Season with salt and pepper.

5 While the sauce is cooking, heat the sugar and vinegar in a small saucepan. Add the chocolate, capers, and olives and cook over low heat until the chocolate has melted. Add to the tomato sauce and cook 5 minutes more.

6 Mix the eggplant and the celery into the tomato sauce. Cook 20 minutes, stirring frequently, so that the flavors of the ingredients can blend together. Pour the caponata into a serving dish and let cool.

7 Pass the hard-boiled eggs through the smallest holes of a vegetable mill, or pushed through a metal strainer. Before serving, cover the caponata with the sieved eggs.

BAGNA CAODA

HOT GARLICKY DIP FOR RAW VEGETABLES

Bagna caôda is a peasant dish from Piedmont, where, in country kitchens, it is made in earthenware pots kept hot on glowing embers. An earthenware pot, small and deep, is indeed by far the best receptacle in which to make it. You will also need a table heater or a candle burner in the middle of the table to keep the bagna caôda hot, though it must not cook. The vegetables are dipped, raw, into the sauce, although some cooks prefer to blanch the cardoons and the celery root.

Plenty of crusty bread and full-bodied red wine, such as a Dolcetto, Barolo, or Nebbiolo, are the other essentials. The oil used should be a mild extra virgin one from Liguria, not a peppery oil from Tuscany.

Serves 4–6

an assortment of raw vegetables such as cardoons, celery, celery root, carrots, radishes, and bell peppers
5 tablespoons butter
5 garlic cloves, very finely sliced or minced
2 ounces salted anchovies, boned, rinsed, and chopped, or canned anchovy fillets, chopped
$\frac{2}{3}$ cup extra virgin olive oil
salt

1 First prepare the vegetables: Cardoons are the traditional vegetable for bagna caôda, but they are not easy to find in this country. If you find some, they will usually already have had their outer leaves and tough stems removed. You will have to remove the strings, as you do with celery stalks. Cut the stalks and the heart into suitable pieces. Rub any cut part with lemon to prevent discoloring. Prepare all the other vegetables as you do for a normal dip, i.e. washing, scraping, stringing, according to the vegetable, and then cutting into fingers. (Celery root will also need a sprinkle of lemon juice to prevent it discoloring.) Choose the best specimens and discard any bruised parts.

2 Melt the butter in a small, deep earthenware pot or a heavy bottomed saucepan over the lowest heat. As soon as the butter has melted and has begun to foam, add the garlic and cook a minute or so. The garlic should not color.

3 Add the anchovies to the pot and pour in the oil very gradually, stirring the whole time. Cook about 10 minutes, always on the lowest possible heat and stirring constantly. The sauce should never come near boiling point. The dip is ready when the anchovies have become a paste. Taste and add salt if necessary. Pepper is not added to traditional bagna caôda.

4 Bring the pot to the table together with the prepared vegetables, and place it over a low flame or on a table heater.

LIST OF RECIPES